SECOND OLDEST

SECOND OLDEST

A Poetic History of Philadelphia

BLYTHE DAVENPORT

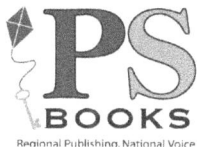

PS
BOOKS
Regional Publishing, National Voice

Second Oldest: A Poetic History of Philadelphia

by Blythe Davenport

The following poems have been published previously:
"Relief" in *Painted Bride Quarterly*; "Commonwealth Brewery,
1925" and "Philly Girls" in *Mad Poets Review*; and "Litter" in
Chronogram Magazine.

ISBN 978-0-9793350-6-8

Cover Image: Jonathan Nitka
Cover Design: Sarah Eldridge

"Front Street at Christian" and "Bartholdi's 'Liberty' Hand and
Torch" from the Free Library of Philadelphia, Print and Picture
Collection, used with permission.

PS Books
93 Old York Road
Ste. 1-753
Jenkintown, PA 19046
www.psbookspublishing.org

for Taylor and Amelia

and for second oldests everywhere

CONTENTS

III.   SPACE WITHIN THESE LINES NOT DEDICATED

Front Street at Christian, 1869

I.   SECOND OLDEST

"The used key is always missing."
                    —Warped Franklin

Dirty River

The smell is as sudden as bad news.
The Delaware ferries
strands of mulched garbage,
harbors boats on both banks—
a war god's game pieces: battleships,
tankers—and is spanned
to the north and south by bridges:
statesman, commander, poet, flag-stitcher.

Man with a Load of Mischief

The man on the Tavern's sign morphed
over the years. First, a young rummy shouldered a
    grinning harlot,
chortling as she piggybacks him; he dropped
her like a bad habit, offered his arm to a finer lady,
and a monkey hopped up on his back.

There was something here before this
dancing sign, the swirl of night
life and liberty tourism:
Delaware tribes once gathered
whortleberries from a copse they called Cooconocon.

There is always something before,
though not always
something after. The ontological
problem we could carry
back and back and still
wonder how god came to be.

Sweltering pools cupped
the nutrients needed for pines
to pop up. And before that

but after
our man relieves himself
of the harpy on his back
and evolves from the harried sinner,
suffering lust, into the swaggering dandy,
no change but time's dig into the sign's weather-cracks.
Still, on Second and Spruce
the man escorts his lady
and steps into the Tavern.

The Gibbet

looks friendly enough
in pictures. When empty, he's quietly ornamental,
arms jaunty akimbo. Flat bands of iron
outline a robotic human form:
two crossed straps bloom into a bulbous head
bolted at the neck
to a swizzle of body circles,
wide at the chest, a stirrup-shaped crotch.

It was forged in 1781 to hold the body
of Thomas Wilkinson.
He was to be hung in gibbets
on Mud Island, a rotting message
to the would-be pirates
navigating the Delaware.

A partial gibbet survives
in Salem, Massachusetts,
used and now clean.
The whole one in Philadelphia
was never filled.

Eastern State Penitentiary, 1871

There's no voice but I know
a tap means place the black sack
over my head. Hands bind
the straps on the back of my neck.
I follow breath and footsteps
down a stone hallway I'd know
even if I saw it. Are there other men
in this prison? Or does this echoing mortar
entomb my small acts
alone? My prayers don't transmit
to a god who only wants to enter me,
not be touched himself.
The prison is mark enough.
An eyeball-shaped window
peers into my cell.
The light shafts in,
a probing finger which pinches
my lips to the cold concrete scream
of the floor. Silence. It says
only, quiet. A shaft of hush.
An accusatory sheerness.

First African Baptist Church Dig

Everything is planted, eventually.
We tickled the ground
with picks and brushes
until it started laughing and laughing
at us. Obscene and wily,
history grinned and tossed
little bits of bone and china,
a leather shoe or two,
and a fistful of coins
then squirmed out of our hands.

I spent the afternoon dusting
all around some teeth and a browbone.
The summer air was a second,
heavy skin in which bobbed
the bulb of the setting sun.
Everything is planted, eventually.

A splinter poked out of the dirt
where no one had yet chiseled; I dug.
She was grinning up
at one hundred and fifty years
of settling dirt. Her head faced west
and her hands palmed her thighs,
and a heavy ceramic plate
covered her chest. The wind why'd and fluffed
dust and bits of bone. This woman,
still a mystery in her dirt mound.

Grumblethorpe Triolet

Grumblethorpe was built in 1744
yet General Agnew's blood still stains the floor;
the Brits moved in during the War.
Grumblethorpe was built in 1744
by a wine merchant named John Wister,
his family's retreat from yellow fever.
Grumblethorpe was built in 1744
now John Agnew's blood still stains the floor.

Congregation of the Dead
(John Adams in Washington Square Park, 1802/2007)

When this was a potter's field, children didn't shriek
and patter after one another in their summer sandals.

Jawbones grin up from below, watching
the fountain spray and woken by the laughter

and footsteps of couples holding hands.
Is there a shriller sound than a child

chasing a butterfly in the middle of a mass
graveyard? Sometimes if a brat leans too far

over the fountain he'll see his own
green and bony skull grinning back.

Zip and chirp of evening birds.
Pink stone home with balcony and balustrade and sky
    blue

gas lamps on each side of the door.
The men whose bones feed the grass

watched the sky star full, the moon swell,
and then they died young of fever or war.

Moving to Susannah's, 1827

My fingers did fine-work,
did rough burlap, did canvas,
stitched the colors of the nation:
blood, indigo, and blank newness.
My pins are tired. Let my daughter lift me up
as these bones drift away, through the city
streets and parks and off
to fight with God once more.
Let Mr. Satterthwaite dig my plot
and grin me into the grave;
a good son-in-law, but he never would
lend my girl even to her mother.

And let the future fly
my draggled gift to history—a flagging memory
is the best we can hope for from patriots,
or from our tip-capping husbands and tippler Friends,
for that matter. That needle bored my skin
as well as the flappy cloth. Holed my bones
straight through, until I gave up
even my home.

Machinery Hall, 1876

It's still a marvel: indoor cataract
splashes, monster machines rear
to attack but heel at men's feet,
rear & heel, rear & heel,
fume sooty breath as dark as their hinges,
spit swift as their longing to bite.
They are tethered to the power source
and shamed by the flutter of women's
hands over their pistons, photographs
of their cowed muscle. They know only light
filtered through the glass ceilings.

Commonwealth Brewery, 1925

Late apples drop into the pub,
harden to cider. Every glass glows
the color of pumpkins and linden leaves.
The crowd is a whisper through trees,
smoke parting lips. The bartender,
hearing nothing, opens the taps.

Brewerytown bobs through the bubbling talks
of factories snapped shut; people
will always need beer, no?
Pride buoys them like the rising sputter
of alcohol from yeast.
They sit at the bar and say, please
don't cut off the tab yet.
You have all I could get.

Girls' High, June 1944

The fresh corsages they carry were hard won
as *don't you know there's a war on*
billets guilt next to their diplomas.
They could be maids of honor in procession,
witnesses to the marriage of pride and duty,
gowned each in white and meshy lace trim.
Slight poof at the shoulder. Demure vee
dips to the bust. They don't smile
as their parents and teachers gather behind
the cameraman, to capture the girls
and their flowers. The principal
ordered them to fold war stamps into blooms:
knock off a Japanazi, for humanity's sake
don't buy German, piece these gluey squares
into red and blue buds. This is a battle they chose:
for an afternoon in June, to be free of war.

Are all cities female,
      or are all women cities?

Philadelphia has ten older sisters. They don't resemble
      her.

Tel Aviv loves to laugh between plosives of anger. She lifts
      her skirts,
suns her ancient port. She only calls Philly when she's
      hungover.
The Mediterranean licks her hips, she hiccups. Her streets
      curve
comb-lines into the coast.

Teutons built a castle around Torun, a prize of old Poland.
      She compares
her son Copernicus to her nephew Franklin, always to
      Ben's detriment.
Murmur her names: Thorun, Turon, Turun, Torn, Thoron,
      Thorn.
I don't work, she says; I'm too old for that. I can't lift red
clay from my riverbanks. My lazy sons chew me through.

Florence tumbles from peak to pit, tries to teach her sister
      patience:
No matter how bloody you get, history will save you. Philly
doesn't believe her: *These are gates of hell, Flo; you've got
      heaven.*

In the Spring and Autumn period, the Duke of Wu dug the
      Grand Canal,
linking the Yangtze to the Huai. The canal birthed Tianjin,
      Philly's straight port sister.
Obedient to the power of her excavation, Tianjin bustles.

Incheon overlooks the Yellow Sea on the northeast corner
    of South Korea's
fetal face. Kobe's wharves creak. The port was busier
    before the quake.
In Russia, Nizhny Novgorod is up to no good, tweaks
    men's mustaches
as they hurry along the cold Prospect. Douala is so
    Littoral; you can't joke
with her. Abruzzo burps abruptly and Aix-en-Provence
    bores.

This is a large family, dotted over the globe.

II.   MUSEUM OF HOAXES

"Diligence is the Mother of Disillusionment."
—Warped Franklin

Bartholdi's "Liberty" Hand and Torch, 1876

Exhibit One

The smoke from a chimney at first
as determined as a flock of birds
heading south, and then disperses
under bad leadership. Each poof
floats its own way and then, as proof
of loss, disappears over the roof.

It looks like some sort of hoax,
the way the chimney smokes
disappear over the oaks.

Cracked Bell

Pass and Stow. Pass and Stow.

The bell-makers' names
preface its life: passed from hand
to hand, bell-tower to steeple, century
to century. Stowed under the floor
of Zion's Reformed Church in Allentown
along with 200 of the city's bells,
so the Brits couldn't melt them for bullets.

The mottled alloy bell, an ugly toad,
squats in many of our stories.
Copper, tin, lead and zinc
with splashes of arsenic and antimony.
We love our symbols of independence,
as any country does; we let them transcend
questionable origins, troublesome history,
even shoddy workmanship.

The Bell never rang
for the Declaration. Never
happened. It's hard to say
it ever rang at all; more of a dull bong.
The State House's bell tower
was so decrepit by 1776
a tug on the bell pull
would bring the whole thing smashing
through the floor.

Merry Weather in Town

It's easy to fall in love
with a city in spring:
whole boulevards of dogwoods in blossom,
double lines of slender
old ladies with shocks
of white curls,
boys with beer on the stoop,
and the sun flexes
his supernova arm, punching
a perfect round brilliant
in the bruised evening sky.

Clinton Street

You'd think this house would hush
laughs with the simple weight
of history; who has stood
by this mantle with one hand
on the marble lip,
head leaning on the cool stone,
Washington? Lafayette?
But it doesn't. A family lives
here, not our city's ghosts.
Those lounge a few blocks east,
arms locked like children in a game
of Red Rover, trying to clothesline
the tourists. At 10th and Clinton,
we sip red wine and fake
living in a million-dollar mansion;
the owners aren't here,
and if they were they'd laugh, too.

Penn's Treaty Tree

The elm is a monster.
It stretches its limbs in swoops,
looms over all the buildings
in Shackamaxon, all the children

shiver as they seesaw and play
on the cold ground under its shadow.
Turned dirt stays moist with no sun,
withery shoots struggle for light.

The elm lies to its visitors,
painters who lay claim to its history.
The tree twists them up in its arms
and slaps broad green leaves

over their mouths and hands.
I know they've been tricked, these
artists who hope we'll believe
the happy version of Penn's treaty.

They hang from the branches, green
gags across their faces, and let the sting
of sharp leaf cut their fingers. They wave
in the breeze. A man in a tri-corner hat

opens his arms in welcome or to offer the trunk
full of beaded belts in trade for land.
Feathers plume on the bald heads
of Indians. Did they really dress in little

triangles of cloth that left them
half bare? A wooden skiff offers escape.
Gourds and plastic bottles roll
around the tree trunk.

Death of the Turkish Automaton

The Holy Roman Empress meets a supernumerary robot,
gift from her cousin, one morning in her court. He holds a
    long, thin pipe
and plays chess; bristles plaster a mustache under
his shellacked nose, squinch as he whispers, *Échec.*
Splayed, he shows only his gears,
continues to conquer. The scam of invisibility
amuses Maria Teresa. His arms buzz and creak,
but the magic of the hand is its sureness, the turban's
controlled menace excites her. Lift a knight,
take a bishop. Maria longs to do both. The hot glow of
    power
grows inside her with only the cool shame of her body to
bury it. She's no machine.

This is just my fable. The fact is fire,
unarguable scorch in Philadelphia's Chinese museum;
the story of the end squashes magic. The brainless
wooden hull, victor against even Napoleon on the
    chessfield,
gobbled flames like a last banquet. Jealous, perhaps, of
    living
kings, blooded queens, and beery bishops,
the robot drank all the heat he could and, though he never
    lived,
death found him tranquil.

The Arm of the Statue of Liberty at the
Centennial Exposition

The giant hand holds her torch on the banks
of the Schuylkill, a coppered Lady
of the Lake. The men built a little Belgian fritte hut,
where they sell tickets to her
forty-two foot climb. They stand next to her, arms on hips,
mugging their own importance
next to the disembodied grasp of idealism.

In a nearby exhibition hall: *The Dreaming Iolanthe*,
a study in butter; just as graspable.

Buried Glass

The slow curl
of blown glass pools
gradual, to gravity's suck.
The bubbles look to pop.
We placed the candy-striped
cane, a dandy's affectation, in your cheap
coffin. Next to your stiff
clasped hands.

No matter how waxed
your parchment skin,
you'll hole up with maggot-tunnels
and melt, down to hollow bone.
I know. I know.
But the colorful swipes
of the glass cane pull slower;
as your skeleton sheds its meat
your cane will hold your soul
with all its tuberant swirls.

70 Sculptors Sitting on the Steps of the PMA, 1949

And I can't name a one. Calder
must be there. They have nice faces: seeing shape
in medium. Each shows his or her hands,
clasped over bent knees, and I wonder
what they've molded: bronze, marble? Animal,
abstraction? A glad formalism
scaffolds the group. Jealousy might lurk, too,
and no one was happy with the mobile's placement
but Calder, but still: they're ready for the 70-seated
dinner table, dotted with 70 goblets of wine.

Relief

What do you do when your sculpture
stares back at you? Poke its eyes,
if it has eyes? Stone pupils don't hurt.

When your statue gazes
with judgment that says
I'll protect you from you
have you done it right or wrong?

The bas relief mastiff on the Fidelity building
hides his nose behind a paw
in frowning disappointment: rough.

Do you reach for your chisel
or change your ways?

Installation

It's not all bronze jesus
and memorials to
generals Pennypacker civil
Tedyuscung chief native debater
negotiator to Penn's men sent
to people the greene towne.
Look around you; the place
works into art on its daily pirouette
commute around city hall pinion
a cotillard of buses zipping
taxis with bikes lacing edges,
detailing busts. Pedestrians step
into the tunic of traffic
rhythmed by red lights.

Dottie's Daughter

The valve opens and spills delicious
beer all over my hands and wrists, golden handcuffs.
I show Billy a picture of Broad Street from on high,
    gossamer
thread glistening into the distance. This is touristy.
I work here, across from Billy Penn's cursed skirts.

Seth flips open his phone with a practiced wrist,
flashes a picture in Eric's face. *Oh, that's*
Dottie's daughter, he knows her but they've never met.
Broken thread—brother sister, boyfriend daughter.
I'm the wife. You're the scissors

snipping. Mika purses her lips, pink
characters in play. I want to call her Maki
but that's a tuna roll. Drumsticks
plick and tap in recorded distance.
Fabric of a smile, costume of a laugh.

I've tricked them: they're having fun
at this round table. Old new, foreign friend.
We thread our way home in a slow taxi. I know
you, he knows me, it's a circle jerk,
blade and pin, bad jokes and good.

I've met Dottie's daughter, and Dottie too.
First a myth of a young brother's love, or to
woo a teenage girl; who knows? My brother
practiced on my sister, left me
grasping the threads of young love.

Moon Tree

The fragrance of the moon
is no sweeter than someone else's child's
tears. This dirt tastes good
veined by the leaky graves
of the hundreds buried under the flagstone paths.
The labor is so far away in space;
the will and work to pull
away from gravity. The anti-entropy
of a seedling placed in a hole
to grow in a potter's field.

Named for Philadelphia

Bonaparte's gull—*Larus Philadelphia*

squawk box rager in the sky
flippy webbed feet pad in the sand
his long beak sniffs your sandwich miles away
swoops in for the steal

Mourning warbler—*Oporornis Philadelphia*

follows the bonaparte's bombast raids with a teary eye
calls, New World Warbler! in his yellow underparts,
gray and olive green feathers
uncertain lilt of his burbling lyrics
a taste for the squishy

Rock Sea Bass—*Centropristis Philadelphia*

What is a centropristis?
Cupped in a puddle of Schuylkill water
metally, cold and fronded with soft algae

Some drunk sploshed in years ago and drowned
now even on a sunny day it's gray by the river

Minute moss beetle and sphecid wasp –
sorry, but they're named for P-A,
but we've got plenty of plants:
the wood lily and Philadelphia fleabane
and our own species of panicum.

Alfredo Cocozza, 1959

"Oh." This was my grandmother.
A tiny, second *h* shirred
her 90-year-old throat.
"Oh*h*, Mario Lanza. What a voice.
My sister made us drive down
to South Philly when they
laid out his body. He was still
a handsome fella."

I don't know if fifty years have shaved
pounds from poor Lanza;
how could anyone's figure survive forty
drumsticks, washed down with a quart of eggnog,
his legendary meals?

Or else the mafia, sometimes accused
of causing Lanza's heart attack,
also planted a fake, beautified body in Philadelphia?
    Because four
black-plumed horses pulled the carriage at Lanza's funeral
in Rome, and they needed every muscle.

Two Times

The Free Library building was once a bank,
still holds the chill of coins
in its stacks. Its arched windows
frame gold clouds, dark-edged
puffs hardened by gilt.
The bronze-rimmed clock clanks
each minute past.

Time flanks my stay at the library,
bonds my life into parcels
that this clock measures
with a cool, crisped note.

Time weighs itself on this city
by the silt built up around cornerstones
dropped into foundations in the 1700s.
Heavy dirt, mudded with history –
not only blood but also arsenic-laced river water,
splattered cement, busted tiles.

III.   SPACE WITHIN THESE LINES NOT DEDICATED

"Love your neighbor, but don't pull down your pants."
—Warped Franklin

Rittenhouse Park

The bench is speckled with birdshit,
Easter candy colors,
chalky and chocolaty bumps.

Twittering finches hop in the grass,
exalt in the pollacking
of the bench. They crow.

Warmth rises, wet and full of
soil and sitting rainwater
that, evaporating, rises slower.

Triangulation with a distant point –
birds, bench, cloud.
Oh unconnected.

Scrub that. The scalene
slides obtuse into a 180.
Flatline.

Strings of ivy shiver in the wind.
Where does that come from?
God's blowhole mouth?

These birds jump, dip and giggle
like baby girls in feathers
of cardinal and magpie.

Traffic brutalizes the park air,
all beeps bloops and twee of birdcall.
Tangerine sun piggybacks the clouds.

The ripped-off street vendor
shrills at a running boy.
Wouldn't it be funny if.

I haven't squealed in pleasure
in years, if ever.

You know they can make flowers
from stone? Realer than the real
thing, though less soft, beautiful and fragrant.

Frog stone, goat bronze, girl
with duck. Fabergé egg information booth,
windows jeweled by the peek-a-boo sun.

Darkling water pond, painted black
to hold the light, warm the coins
that speckle the bottom.

Kelly Drive

Old family skeletons greet their daily horrors
behind coppered plaques,
in great marble halls,

on Laurel Hill. Joggers
in bright terrycloth chuff by, unaware

of the dark in the mausoleums,
the chafe of dusty time

on marbleizing flesh.
Runners breathe in the wet, mud-fresh air.

They jog their meaty legs
and pump their lungs.

They run to become skeletons
in less dignified homes.

To Philadelphia

The stretch between Pittsburgh
and Philadelphia runs about two hundred
and ninety-seven miles.

The trees are all outlined in cold white,
and leafless, like root systems
long-sprouted the wrong way.

You're a Marine, but you're all
little boys in the morning,
in boxers in the bathroom barefoot.

You're a Marine, something I've always equated
with the aquatic, a deep green
in the ocean.

The April soil is brown
as cider and ready for seeding.

Shade and Danger

Silver-sided trains
back-and-forth through Suburban Station
like polished pistons stretched immense.

I'm awful below
cherry blossomed streets

++

The blank mind at the end of a tired day
echoes, *There's no reason why*
There's no reason why you should act strange
like the young man in the tunnel
until I turned the corner into the tsk-us, discus
hiss of the drummer and his whisk.

Snowing

The background is a flat slap
of dun row houses, shaded over
by the fuzzy gray of snowcloud.
Pointing up: telephone poles;
the twelve-fingered hand
of a bare tree; a chimney.
The windows, clapped on walls
like paper, gape at the April flurry.

City Hall Tower

The elevator fits four and five
people are packed in, slowly rising forty floors.
Our operator fills the cabin
with boozy breath. We glide past millions of bricks.
The tower clocks are tiny gears
with big flat faces to the city,
eyeballing each direction.

Elevator man wants to live in Georgia. Arkansas
tourist talks up retirement in Mexico,
where bartenders hop to a two-dollar tip.
I'm fine here in the north. A river of Listerine
floods the elevator as we wobble to a stop.
Masonry doesn't sway?

Broad Street ramrods south to north, pistons City Hall.
The Delaware and Schuylkill rivers
curl around east and west. Windows open all around and
   up,
open sky filled by a thirty-seven-foot tall Billy Penn.

His big bronze palm pats me down.
Calm, calm, it says. He holds the charter
to the once-woody land he surveys.
I follow his gaze. "Eggar Allan Poe
s'got a house up there,"
mumbles my lubed elevator
friend, as if North Philadelphia were a favorite
vacation spot for the gothic dead.

From here the killing neighborhoods
are orderly as drawn plans; I'd buy.

Allegheny Avenue, 2007

The loading docks, mouths agape,
gum the empty street below the broken-eye
windows. I walk along the tracks
past old paper mills, belt factories, smoke stacks
cleaned out by disuse. The ball bearing
clacks in my spray cans, mixes the liquids
that I use to color this neighborhood.
The sky, gray as lead and heavy, pools
down around the brick towers.
It's all piling up.

My voice is wrong. My voice doesn't waver
around these husks that were so big
when I was small. I could smash
them now with one swift kick.
The gray sky doesn't bother me much.
I just want to shake the clacker,
wrap my fingers around the cylinder,
the cool that slips past the thin aluminum,
and press the stopper to spray out a hiss of gas-color.
First dusting pulls on more particles
as color piles on color, line
on stream on puddle.
The track is loneliness underlining itself,
leads past Sydenham and Lippincott Streets, the dead
ends that butt up on the slash of tracks,
the broke eyeball of the sun.
The air tastes like the tracks, metal cold.
The clacker clacks.

Bruised

Today I'm on the phone
with a friend who is fresh
out of the hospital. The full bloom
fungus twills a purple burst,
bruises the innocent, already hacked-off stump.
He's suffered enough, torn in half,
and this upstart contusion
overshadows him. It's the business tip of the iceberg
that plows the hull open, spilling tidal frost
where oiled machines should go, planting doom.

The dense circled stump
trumps the moist ground
only slightly. The wood is as wet
as the soil, a deep maroon
fungus frills out of the shorn tree,
preening its august fineness,
enjoying the hint of winter
on dying summer air.
The wind is freighted with exhaust
that curls in through the gate
of the small street-side park.

Bastard bloom, schizo
mushroom scab. I do love you
for your deep color, your debonair growth,
where only rot will sink
in. So full, so plump,
burst your stump for its nutrients
and show the stringy vine of ivy
how it's done: low to the ground, wide sweep,
no need to cling and climb an already defined height.
Someone has been there, done that wall,
so that ivy's million tiny fingers
can pull it down. It all goes
around and around.

Chestnut Street Park

A man taps a new pack of smokes,
lights up, coughs
in counterpoint to the delivery trucks'
chug-chug putter on Chestnut.
It's neat, this little pocket
of pocked concrete
where I eat lunch on summer days,
when the fountain still burbles over
its squared towers. It quiets in September, and
little tips of sidewalk
conversations spill into the stiller air,
moments shared, borrowed, enough
to keep me company
when I don't want my own.

Laurel Hill

This morning in the cemetery I snapped
a half-dozen shots of ruined graves.
One long, flat stone,
engraved "I look toward the resurrection of the dead"
had been burrowed under, or out of; a hand-shaped hole
peered unblinking as the dead
back at my lens. Obelisks rose
all around me, pointing the way
to heaven for any of those souls
disoriented by their recent tumble
and whirl from life, to coffin, to earth.
The tallest one closest to god.

Love Park

In winter, this fountain is quiet,
a wide-open, dry eye.
But on a perfect autumn afternoon
like today, the sun
ripens from horizon to apex,
pale to dark, like fresh watermelon on its rind.
Tunes blast from a nearby stage,
arguing with the tall white finger
of the fountain's blasting waters.
Funk. Tom Petty.
The fountain awake.
Oh my my
The waters pointing.
Oh hell yes
Up, up, up.

Hidden River

My coat picks up fry-smell
from the corner lunchcart
and lugs it down the block, grease-heavy.
Onions peppers beef.
The concrete sidewalk, speckled ugly
as my face, pocked and dirty.

The narrow river of blue that runs
between buildings above Market.
Clouds whisper from the edge
of one rooftop to another.

This is a good town. You can tell
by the loser sports teams
and that fry-up air
that keeps bums fed
by breathing it.
Warmth fogs out of sidewalk grates
housing shoeless joes,
asleep and urinous.
No wonder everyone smokes—another sign
of a good town.

Litter

I sometimes envy the evidence of languid hours:
a congregation of acrid filters
commiserating beneath a bench;
the front stoop caped
in feathers of newspaper;
shards of green longnecks
freckling the cement.
Until I had sluiced bluesmoke to
mine coal stripes in my pink lungs,
or smashed bottles, pissed incontinent,
between cars and curbs,
I interpreted litter
with thick-lipped innocence.
Now I smile while walking by,
same mouth, just stained.

Philly Girls

Philly girls look both ways: they look you up
and down. They look both sweet and hard –
rock candy. They sling schoolgirl skirts
over women's hips, bounce ponytails
over slangy, smoky lips. They stroll by,
loud and laughing. Some have mustaches
and frizzy hair. Some are the best-dressed ladies,
on or off food stamps.
Some are paunchy from beer and peanuts
or a pregnancy that seemed, for its first five minutes,
a good idea.

Rundown

On summer evenings, a walk through
North Philly streets is an exercise
in creature-sighting; you'll find only ghosts.
They sway the yellow leaves
and whir in alleys, whistle the window shards
on rundown townhouses.

Rundown cuddles street corners
and stults the city into collapsing parts.

You may see hackies maze their cabs
down 13th to manurish stables,
maundering in a haze of fumes.
Left on the corner
an old man gives you the rundown,
hawking his hagiography: a mass
of imprisoned beauties
and the alphabet of their habits,
souls that now flap the plastic
lapidating the window frames.
They count the age of the earth
by how much salt in the sea,
how much erosion of their city.

Abandoned North Broad

Windows are cross-hatched with metal
wire, protecting a sign that reads,
"This is not the prison society."

A crop of lofts, and for-sale
signs sprouting from buildingsides
might remake this road
to the ghetto.

Walk it today
for a tour from the twenties
through the international style
and stilt at the eighties.

Self-Immolation 2
for Kathy Change

A gust of water,
skin peeling like chiffon
robes from my body

Trachea tunnel
glottals sunshine

Nothing but a skip
in the family book
the human history

and just a toenail, scrabble claw
of fire's saga—long-forgotten
queens and goddesses

I'm looking for long-gone
ashes

Acknowledgments

I'd like to thank these publications, and their editors, for their early acceptance of the following pieces: *Painted Bride Quarterly* ("Relief"); *Mad Poets Review* ("Commonwealth Brewery, 1925" and "Philly Girls"); and *Chronogram Magazine* ("Litter").

I also want to thank the kind people who read and supported my efforts, without whom this book would not be—especially my amazing husband, Eric; Liz Abrams-Morley; and the fabulous Courtney Bambrick. Special acknowledgments to Carla Spataro and Michelle Wittle for their patience and guidance. And my most sincere gratitude goes to the Poetry Free-for-all, where I started learning the craft of poetry thirteen years ago.

www.ingramcontent.com/pod-product-compliance
Lightning Source LLC
Chambersburg PA
CBHW071242090426
42736CB00014B/3180

* 9 7 8 0 9 7 9 3 3 5 0 6 8 *